63rd Annual Meeting of the Association for Computational Linguistics (ACL 2025)

Tutorial Abstracts

Vienna, Austria
27 July 2025

ISBN: 979-8-3313-2392-9

Printed from e-media with permission by:

Curran Associates, Inc.
57 Morehouse Lane
Red Hook, NY 12571

CURRAN ASSOCIATES INC. proceedings.com

Some format issues inherent in the e-media version may also appear in this print version.

Association for Computational Linguistics
209 N. Eighth Street
Stroudsburg, Pennsylvania 18360

Phone: 1-570-476-8006
Fax: 1-570-476-0860

acl@aclweb.org

Additional copies of this publication are available from:

Curran Associates, Inc.
57 Morehouse Lane
Red Hook, NY 12571 USA
Phone: 845-758-0400
Fax: 845-758-2633
Email: curran@proceedings.com
Web: www.proceedings.com

ACL 2025

The 63rd Annual Meeting of the Association for Computational Linguistics

Tutorial Abstracts

July 27, 2025

Introduction

Welcome to the tutorial session of ACL 2025!

We are thrilled to welcome you to this year's ACL tutorial session, a cornerstone event of the conference. Our tutorials offer a deep dive into a diverse range of cutting-edge and emerging topics, presented by leading researchers at the forefront of their fields. These sessions are designed to equip you with the latest insights, tools, and methodologies, enriching your understanding of the ever-evolving landscape of computational linguistics and natural language processing.

Continuing our longstanding tradition, the call, submission, review, and selection processes for tutorials were jointly coordinated across NAACL, ACL, and EMNLP. The review committee comprised the NAACL tutorial chairs (Rui Zhang, Swabha Swayamdipta, and Maria Lomeli), the ACL tutorial chairs (Yuki Arase, David Jurgens, and Fei Xia), and EMNLP tutorial representatives (Jessy Li and Fei Liu). Each tutorial proposal underwent a thorough evaluation by a panel of two to three reviewers, who assessed the submissions based on several key criteria: clarity and preparedness, novelty and timeliness of the topic, instructors' experience, anticipated audience interest, commitment to open access teaching materials, and diversity considerations—including multilingualism, gender, age, and geographic representation—as well as compatibility with the preferred conference venue. The tutorial chairs for all three conferences met to dicsuss each tutorial and make the final decisions and assignments to each conference.

This year, we received a remarkable total of 76 tutorial submissions, many of which were very engaging and made for a highly competitive selection process. Ultimately, 8 tutorials were selected for presentation at ACL. These tutorials promise to offer engaging and informative sessions, catering to a broad spectrum of interests and expertise levels within the computational linguistics and NLP community.

We deeply appreciate the contributions of all tutorial authors, as well as the tireless efforts and strong collaboration of the conference organizers—with special thanks to General Chair Roberto Navigli for his exceptional leadership and Jenn Rachford for her work in scheduling and coordinating tutorials at the conference.

We hope these tutorials provide an exciting and engaging start to your overall experience at ACL 2025. Wishing you an inspiring and engaging time at the conference, filled with learning and connection!

Warm regards,
ACL 2025 Tutorial Co-Chairs,
Yuki Arase, David Jurgens, and Fei Xia

Organizing Committee

General Chair

Roberto Navigli, Sapienza University Rome & Babelscape

Program Chairs

Wanxiang Che, Harbin Institute of Technology
Joyce Nabende, Makerere University
Ekaterina Shutova, University of Amsterdam
Mohammad Taher Pilehvar, Cardiff University / Tehran Institute for Advanced Studies

Tutorial Chairs

Yuki Arase, Tokyo Institute of Technology
David Jurgens, University of Michigan
Fei Xia, University of Washington

Table of Contents

Program

Sunday, July 27, 2025

09:00 - 12:30	*Inverse Reinforcement Learning Meets Large Language Model Alignment*
09:00 - 12:30	*Eye Tracking and NLP*
09:00 - 12:30	*Uncertainty Quantification for Large Language Models*
09:00 - 12:30	*Human-AI Collaboration: How AIs Augment Human Teammates*
14:00 - 12:30	*Break*
14:00 - 17:30	*Navigating Ethical Challenges in NLP: Hands-on strategies for students and researchers*
14:00 - 17:30	*NLP for Counterspeech against Hate and Misinformation*
14:00 - 17:30	*Synthetic Data in the Era of Large Language Models*
14:00 - 17:30	*Guardrails and Security for LLMs: Safe, Secure, and Controllable Steering of LLM Applications*

Inverse Reinforcement Learning Meets Large Language Model Alignment

Mihaela van der Schaar and Hao Sun

Website: `https://sites.google.com/view/irl-llm`

In the era of Large Language Models (LLMs), alignment has emerged as a fundamental yet challenging problem in the pursuit of more reliable, controllable, and capable machine intelligence. The recent success of reasoning models and conversational AI systems has underscored the critical role of reinforcement learning (RL) in enhancing these systems, driving increased research interest at the intersection of RL and LLM alignment.

This tutorial will provide a comprehensive review of recent advances in LLM alignment through the lens of inverse reinforcement learning (IRL), emphasizing the distinctions between RL techniques employed in LLM alignment and those in conventional RL tasks. In particular, we highlight the necessity of constructing neural reward models from human data and discuss the formal and practical implications of this paradigm shift. The tutorial will begin with fundamental concepts in RL to provide a foundation for the audience unfamiliar with the field. We then examine recent advances in this research agenda, discussing key challenges and opportunities in conducting IRL for LLM alignment. Beyond methodological considerations, we explore practical aspects, including datasets, benchmarks, evaluation metrics, infrastructure, and computationally efficient training and inference techniques.

Finally, we draw insights from the literature on sparse-reward RL to identify open questions and potential research directions. By synthesizing findings from diverse studies, we aim to provide a structured and critical overview of the field, highlight unresolved challenges, and outline promising future directions for improving LLM alignment through RL and IRL techniques.

Mihaela van der Schaar, Professor, University of Cambridge
Email: `mv472@cam.ac.uk`
Website: `https://www.vanderschaar-lab.com/prof-mihaela-van-der-schaar/`

Professor Mihaela van der Schaar is the John Humphrey Plummer Professor of Machine Learning, Artificial Intelligence, and Medicine at the University of Cambridge, where she leads the van der Schaar Lab and directs the Cambridge Centre for AI in Medicine (CCAIM). She is a Fellow of the IEEE (2009) and of the Royal Society (2024), and has received numerous accolades, including the Johann Anton Merck Award (2024), the Oon Prize for Preventative Medicine (2018), and the NSF CAREER Award (2004). A former Turing Fellow (2016–2024), she was named Spinoza Guest Professor at Amsterdam UMC in 2025.

Hao Sun, PhD student, University of Cambridge
Email: `hs789@cam.ac.uk`
Website: `https://holarissun.github.io/`

Hao Sun is a 4th-year PhD at the University of Cambridge, specializing in RL and LLM alignment. Hao's research in RL has been published at NeurIPS, covering the topics of sparse-reward RL, reward shaping and design, exploration and exploitation, and interpretability. Hao's research on LLM alignment focuses on building reward models from diverse data sources using an Inverse RL framework, and has led to publications at ICLR, ICML, and ACL, and contributed to a tutorial series at AAAI 2025 and ACL 2025.

Proceedings of the 63rd Annual Meeting of the Association for Computational Linguistics (Volume 5: Tutorial Abstracts), pages 1–1
July 27, 2025

Eye Tracking and NLP

David Reich, Omer Shubi, Lena Jäger and Yevgeni Berzak

Website: https://acl2025-eyetracking-and-nlp.github.io/

Our tutorial introduces a growing research area that combines eye tracking during reading with NLP. The tutorial outlines how eye movements in reading can be leveraged for NLP, and, vice versa, how NLP methods can advance psycholinguistic modeling of eye movements in reading. We cover four main themes: (i) fundamentals of eye movements in reading, (ii) experimental methodologies and available data, (iii) integrating eye movement data in NLP models, and (iv) using LLMs for modeling eye movements in reading. The tutorial is tailored to NLP researchers and practitioners, and provides the essential background for conducting research on joint modeling of eye movements and text.

David Reich, PhD student, University of Potsdam and University of Zurich.
Email: david.reich@uni-potsdam.de
Website: https://www.cl.uzh.ch/en/research-groups/digital-linguistics/people/lab-members/reich.html
My research interests span applied machine learning, NLP, and eyetracking. My current focus is on generative models for eye-tracking data.

Omer Shubi, PhD student, Technion - Israel Institute of Technology.
Email: shubi@campus.technion.ac.il
Website: https://omershubi.github.io/
My research interests are at the intersection of NLP, psycholinguistics and cognitive science, with a focus on analyzing and decoding cognitive state in language comprehension from eye movements.

Lena Jäger, Associate Professor, University of Zurich.
Email: lenaann.jaeger@uzh.ch
Website: https://www.cl.uzh.ch/en/research-groups/digital-linguistics/people/group-leader/jaeger.html
My research interests lie at the intersection of experimental and computational psycholinguistics, machine learning and NLP. The focus of my current research is the development of methods for leveraging eyetracking data for a broad range of language-related use cases, such as gaze-augmented language modeling, the inference of an individual's reading comprehension or foreign language skills, or the development of generative models to simulate human eye movements in reading. I am currently leading the EU COST Action MultiplEYE, an international network of researchers focusing on collecting and using multilingual eyetracking-while-reading data for computational psycholingusitics and NLP.

Yevgeni Berzak, Assistant Professor, Technion - Israel Institute of Technology.
Email: berzak@technion.ac.il
Website: https://lacclab.github.io/
My research lies on the intersection of Cognitive Science and Natural Language Processing (NLP). I study how humans acquire and process language by combining linguistic and cognitive theory, computational modeling, and behavioral and neuroimaging studies. I also examine how natural language processing in machines can be brought closer to human linguistic abilities by using insights and data from human language processing.

Proceedings of the 63rd Annual Meeting of the Association for Computational Linguistics (Volume 5: Tutorial Abstracts), pages 2–2
July 27, 2025 ©2025 Association for Computational Linguistics

Uncertainty Quantification for Large Language Models

Artem Shelmanov, Maxim Panov, Roman Vashurin,
Artem Vazhentsev, Ekaterina Fadeeva, and Timothy Baldwin

Website: `http://uncertainty-for-llm.nlpresearch.group`

Large language models (LLMs) are widely used in NLP applications, but their tendency to produce hallucinations poses significant challenges to the reliability and safety, ultimately undermining user trust. This tutorial offers the first systematic introduction to uncertainty quantification (UQ) for LLMs in text generation tasks – a conceptual and methodological framework that provides tools for communicating the reliability of a model answer. This additional output could be leveraged for a range of downstream tasks, including hallucination detection and selective generation. We begin with the theoretical foundations of uncertainty, highlighting why techniques developed for classification might fall short in text generation. Building on this grounding, we survey state-of-the-art white-box and black-box UQ methods, from simple entropy-based scores to supervised probes over hidden states and attention weights, and show how they enable selective generation and hallucination detection. Additionally, we discuss the calibration of uncertainty scores for better interpretability. A key feature of the tutorial is practical examples using LM-Polygraph, an open-source framework that unifies more than a dozen recent UQ and calibration algorithms and provides a large-scale benchmark, allowing participants to implement UQ in their applications, as well as reproduce and extend experimental results with only a few lines of code. By the end of the session, researchers and practitioners will be equipped to (i) evaluate and compare existing UQ techniques, (ii) develop new methods, and (iii) implement UQ in their code for deploying safer, more trustworthy LLM-based systems.

Artem Shelmanov, Senior Research Scientist at MBZUAI, UAE.
Email: `artem.shelmanov@mbzuai.ac.ae`
Website: `https://iinemo.github.io`

Dr. Artem Shelmanov leads a research team focused on debiasing, hallucination detection, and uncertainty quantification methods for LLMs. His team has developed a series of robust UQ techniques for text classification models and generative LLMs, as well as a series of active learning algorithms for various NLP tasks. Dr. Artem leads the development of LM-Polygraph – one of the most comprehensive Python libraries for uncertainty quantification and hallucination detection in LLMs. He is also one of the organizers of the UncertainNLP workshop at EMNLP-2025.

Maxim Panov, Assistant Professor at MBZUAI, UAE.
Email: `maxim.panov@mbzuai.ac.ae`
Website: `https://mbzuai.ac.ae/study/faculty/maxim-panov/`

Maxim Panov's research is focused on uncertainty quantification for machine learning model predictions and Bayesian approaches to machine learning. In particular, Maxim's research group works on hallucination detection for LLMs. Maxim also co-leads the development of the LM-Polygraph library.

Roman Vashurin, Senior Research Engineer at MBZUAI, UAE.
Email: roman.vashurin@mbzuai.ac.ae

Roman Vashurin conducts research on uncertainty quantification in LLMs with a focus on unsupervised and semi-supervised approaches, developing new and extensively benchmarking existing methods. Roman is one of the core developers of the LM-Polygraph library.

Proceedings of the 63rd Annual Meeting of the Association for Computational Linguistics (Volume 5: Tutorial Abstracts), pages 3–4
July 27, 2025 ©2025 Association for Computational Linguistics

Artem Vazhentsev, PhD student at Skoltech and a researcher at AIRI.
Email: vazhentsev@airi.net
Artem Vazhentsev works on novel uncertainty quantification methods for LLMs and other NLP models. Artem developed several density-based and attention-based supervised UQ methods for text generation and classification models. He is one of the core developers of the LM-Polygraph library.

Ekaterina Fadeeva, PhD student at the LRE Lab, Department of Computer Science, ETH Zürich, Switzerland.
Email: efadeeva@ethz.ch
Ekaterina Fadeeva's research focuses on uncertainty quantification for LLMs, with applications to claim-level hallucination detection and reasoning models. She is one of the core developers of the LM-Polygraph library.

Timothy Baldwin, Provost, Professor at MBZUAI, UAE.
Email: timothy.baldwin@mbzuai.ac.ae
Website: https://mbzuai.ac.ae/study/faculty/timothy-baldwin/
Tim Baldwin is a full Professor in the Natural Language Processing department and Provost of MBZUAI, as well as a Melbourne Laureate Professor at The University of Melbourne. He was also the President of the Association for Computational Linguistics in 2022. His research interests encompass natural language processing, algorithmic fairness, AI safety, and computational social science. Tim has authored a series of publications related to uncertainty quantification and the interaction between debiasing and UQ techniques. He leads several projects focused on enhancing the safety and trustworthiness of LLMs.

Human-AI Collaboration: How AIs Augment Human Teammates

Tongshuang Wu, Diyi Yang, Joseph Chang, Marti A. Hearst, and Kyle Lo

Website: `https://acl25-hai-team.github.io/`

The continuous, rapid development of general- purpose models like LLMs suggests the theoretical possibility of AI performing any human task. Yet, despite the potential and promise, these models are far from perfect, excelling at certain tasks while struggling with others. The tension between what is possible and a model's limitations raises the general research question that has attracted attention from various disciplines: What is the best way to use AI to maximize its benefits? In this tutorial, we will review recent developments related to human-AI teaming and collaboration. To the best of our knowledge, our tutorial will be the first to provide a more integrated view from NLP, HCI, Computational Social Science, and Learning Science, etc., and highlight how different communities have identified the goals and societal impacts of such collaborations, both positive and negative. We will further discuss how to operationalize these Human-AI collaboration goals, and reflect on how state-of-the-art AI models should be evaluated and scaffolded to make them most useful in collaborative contexts.

Sherry Wu, Assistant Professor, Carnegie Mellon University
Email: `sherryw@cs.cmu.edu`
Website: `http://cs.cmu.edu/~sherryw`
Sherry Wu is an assistant professor at the Human-Computer Interaction Institute, Carnegie Mellon University. Her primary research investigates how humans (AI experts, lay users, domain experts) interact with (debug, audit, and collaborate) AI systems. Sherry has organized two workshops at NLP and HCI conferences: Shared Stories and Lessons Learned workshop at EMNLP 2022 and Trust and Reliance in AI-Human Teams at CHI 2022 and 2023. She has given two well-received tutorials relevant to Human-AI Interaction, one at EMNLP 2023 on Designing, Learning from, and Evaluating Human-AI Interactions, and another one on Human-AI Interactions in the Era of LLMs at NAACL 2024.

Diyi Yang, Assistant Professor, Stanford University
Email: `diyiy@stanford.edu`
Website: `https://cs.stanford.edu/~diyiy/`
Diyi Yang is an assistant professor in the Computer Science Department at Stanford University. Her research focuses on human-centered natural language processing and computational social science. Diyi has organized four workshops at NLP conferences: Widening NLP Workshops at NAACL 2018 and ACL 2019, Casual Inference workshop at EMNLP 2021, NLG Evaluation workshop at EMNLP 2021, and Shared Stories and Lessons Learned workshop at EMNLP 2022. She also gave a tutorial at ACL 2022 on Learning with Limited Data, and a tutorial at EACL 2023 on Summarizing Conversations at Scale. Diyi and Sherry have co-developed a new course on Human-Centered NLP that has been offered at both Stanford and CMU.

Joseph Chee Chang, Research Scientist, AI2
Email: `josephc@allenai.org`
Website: `https://joe.cat/`
Joseph Chee Chang is a research scientist at the Allen Institute for AI, where he study and design novel Human-AI systems and user interfaces to facilitate sensemaking. His recent projects include interactive human-agent planning and execution, intelligent and interactive reading interfaces for scholarly documents, and other research support tools including systems

Proceedings of the 63rd Annual Meeting of the Association for Computational Linguistics (Volume 5: Tutorial Abstracts), pages 5–6
July 27, 2025 ©2025 Association for Computational Linguistics

for ideation and literature review.

Marti A. Hearst, Professor, UC Berkeley
Email: hearst@berkeley.edu
Website: https://people.ischool.berkeley.edu/~hearst/
Marti A. Hearst is a professor and the Interim Dean for the UC Berkeley School of Information. She is both an ACL Fellow and a SIGCHI Academy member, and former ACL President. Her research has long combined HCI and NLP; recent projects include adding interactivity to scholarly documents and creating interactive newspods. She recently gave invited keynote talks at the EACL NLP + HCI workshop, the KDD Workshop on Data Science with a Human in the Loop, and she advised the 2022 NAACL program chairs on the Human-Centered Natural Language Processing special theme. She has taught courses in NLP, HCI, and information visualization for 25 years.

Kyle Lo, Research Scientist, AI2
Email: kylel@allenai.org
Website: https://kyleclo.com/
Kyle Lo is a research scientist at the Allen Institute for AI working on natural language processing, machine learning and human-AI interaction, with emphasis on the impact of training data on model behavior, evaluation methodology, and intelligent reading interfaces. Kyle has organized four workshops on NLP for scholarly documents, including at NAACL 2021, COLING 2022 and AKBC 2020-2021, as well as three shared tasks on scientific information retrieval and fact checking at TREC 2021 and TAC 2020. Kyle also presented a tutorial on language model development at NeurIPS 2024.

Navigating Ethical Challenges in NLP: Hands-on strategies for students and researchers

Luciana Benotti, Fanny Ducel, Karën Fort, Guido Ivetta, Zhijing Jin, Min-Yen Kan, Seunghun J. Lee, Margot Mieskes, Minzhi Li, and Adriana Pagano

Website: https://ethics.aclweb.org/tutorials/ACL_2025/

With NLP research being rapidly productionized into real-world applications, it is important to be aware of and think through the consequences of our work. Such ethical considerations are important in both authoring and reviewing (e.g. privacy, consent, fairness, among others).

This tutorial will equip participants with basic guidelines for thinking deeply about ethical issues and review common considerations that recur in NLP research. The methodology is interactive and participatory, including discussion of case studies and group work. Participants will gain practical experience on when to flag a paper for ethics review and how to write an ethical consideration section to be shared with the broader community. Most importantly, the participants will be co-creating the tutorial outcomes and extending tutorial materials to share as public outcomes.

Luciana Benotti, Associate Professor, Universidad Nacional de Córdoba
Email: `luciana.benotti@unc.edu.ar`
Website: `https://benotti.github.io/`
Luciana Benotti is an Associate Professor at the Universidad Nacional de Córdoba, Argentina. Her research interests include situated and grounded language, especially the study of misunderstandings, bias, stereotypes, and clarification requests. She is a co-chair of the ACL ethics committee.

Fanny Ducel, PhD Candidate, Université Paris-Saclay
Email: `fanny.ducel@universite-paris-saclay.fr`
Website: `https://fannyducel.github.io/`
Fanny Ducel is a PhD candidate at the Université Paris-Saclay, France. She works on stereotypical biases in LLMs. She also teaches ethics to international NLP graduates.

Karën Fort, Professor, Université de Lorraine
Email: `karen.fort@loria.fr`
Website: `https://members.loria.fr/KFort/`
Karën Fort is a Professor at the Université de Lorraine, France. She has been working on ethics and teaching ethics in NLP since 2014. She was co-chair of the first two ethics committees in the field, in 2020 and 2021, and is co-chair of the ACL ethics committee.

Guido Ivetta, PhD Candidate, Universidad Nacional de Córdoba
Email: `guidoivetta@unc.edu.ar`
Website: `https://guidoivetta.github.io/`
Guido Ivetta is a PhD candidate at the Universidad Nacional de Córdoba, Argentina. His work focuses on language model calibration and biases. He teaches AI ethics to K–12 teachers.

Zhijing Jin, Incoming Assistant Professor, University of Toronto
Email: `zjin@cs.toronto.edu`
Website: `https://zhijing-jin.com/`
Zhijing Jin is an incoming Assistant Professor at the University of Toronto, and currently a postdoc at the Max Planck Institute in Germany. Her research focuses on Causality for NLP

Proceedings of the 63rd Annual Meeting of the Association for Computational Linguistics (Volume 5: Tutorial Abstracts), pages 7–8
July 27, 2025 ©2025 Association for Computational Linguistics

and NLP for Social Good. She has co-organized many workshops (e.g., several NLP for Positive Impact Workshops at ACL and EMNLP, and Causal Representation Learning Workshop at NeurIPS 2024), and also the ACL Year-Round Mentorship since 2021.

Min-Yen Kan, Associate Professor, National University of Singapore
Email: `kanmy@comp.nus.edu.sg`
Website: `https://www.comp.nus.edu.sg/~kanmy/`
Min-Yen Kan is an Associate Professor at the National University of Singapore and a co-chair of the ACL ethics committee. He was a previous member of the ACL executive committee, the inaugural Information Officer, and a previous ACL Anthology Director.

Seunghun J. Lee, Senior Associate Professor, International Christian University
Email: `seunghun@icu.ac.jp`
Website: `https://sites.google.com/view/seunghunjlee/home`
Seunghun J. Lee is a Senior Associate Professor of Linguistics at the International Christian University, a liberal arts college in Tokyo, Japan. He is also an Adjunct Professor of African Languages at the University of Venda in South Africa, and an Honorary Associate Professor in the Centre for Linguistic Science and Technology at the Indian Institute of Technology Guwahati in India.

Minzhi Li, PhD Candidate, National University of Singapore
Email: `li.minzhi@u.nus.edu`
Website: `https://yocodeyo.github.io/`
Minzhi Li is a PhD candidate at the National University of Singapore. Her main research interest is socially aware NLP.

Margot Mieskes, Professor, University of Applied Sciences Darmstadt
Email: `margot.mieskes@h-da.de`
Website: `https://sis.h-da.de/personen/professor-innen-auf-einen-blick/prof-dr-margot-mieskes`
Margot Mieskes is a Professor for Information Science at the University of Applied Sciences, Darmstadt, Germany. She works in Computational Linguistics (CL) and Natural Language Processing (NLP), focusing on automatic summarization, evaluation methods, data quality, emotion detection, ethics, experiment reproducibility, and biases in large language models.

Adriana Pagano, Full Professor, Federal University of Minas Gerais
Email: `apagano@ufmg.br`
Website: `https://scholar.google.com.br/citations?user=iMOX_EQAAAAJ`
Adriana Pagano is a Full Professor in Applied Linguistics at the Federal University of Minas Gerais, Brazil, where she supervises MA and PhD students in Applied and Computational Linguistics. She is a Research Fellow of the National Council for Scientific and Technological Development (CNPq) and the Minas Gerais State Agency for Research and Development (FAPEMIG), pursuing studies on multilingual text production and modeling. She is currently leading an international interdisciplinary project on benchmarking LLMs for Responsible AI. She is a member of the Ethics Committee for AI at the Federal University of Minas Gerais.

NLP for Counterspeech against Hate and Misinformation (CSHAM)

Daniel Russo, Helena Bonaldi, Yi-Ling Chung, Gavin Abercrombie and Marco Guerini
Invited speakers: Cathy Buerger and Simone Fontana

Website: https://sites.google.com/view/nlp4csham

This tutorial aims to bring together research from different fields such as computer science and the social sciences and policy to show how counterspeech is currently used to tackle abuse and misinformation by individuals, activists and organisations, how Natural Language Processing (NLP) and Generation (NLG) can be applied to automate its production, and the implications of using large language models for this task. It will also address, but not be limited to, the questions of how to evaluate and measure the impacts of counterspeech, the importance of expert knowledge from civil society in the development of counterspeech datasets and taxonomies, and how to ensure fairness and mitigate the biases present in language models when generating counterspeech.

The tutorial will bring diverse multidisciplinary perspectives to safety research by including case studies from industry and public policy to share insights on the impact of counterspeech and social correction and the implications of applying NLP to critical real-world problems. It will also go deeper into the challenging task of tackling hate and misinformation together, which represents an open research question yet to be addressed in NLP but gaining attention as a stand alone topic.

---

(1) Presenters:

Daniel Russo, PhD Student at University of Trento and Fondazione Bruno Kessler, Italy.
Email: drusso@fbk.eu
Website: https://drusso98.github.io/
Daniel Russo is undertaking a PhD in the field of natural language generation at the University of Trento, Italy, in collaboration with Fondazione Bruno Kessler, under the supervision of Marco Guerini. Here, he is a member of the Language and Dialogue Technologies Group. He holds an MSc in Cognitive Science and a BSc in Computer Science. He co-organised the PoliticIT shared task at the EVALITA 2023 Italian Evaluation Campaign. His principal research interest is the automatic countering of online misinformation.

Helena Bonaldi, PhD Student at University of Trento and Fondazione Bruno Kessler, Italy.
Email: hbonaldi@fbk.eu
Website: https://helenabon.github.io/
Helena Bonaldi is a PhD student in the LanD group at Fondazione Bruno Kessler, under the supervision of Marco Guerini. Her research mainly focuses on the automatic generation of counterspeech against hate. Recently, she has started investigating the intersection of hate and misinformation in the context of the Hatedemics project. She has co-organised the Counterspeech for Online abuse (CS4OA) and the Multilingual Counterspeech Generation workshops.

Yi-Ling Chung, Senior research scientist, Genaios
Email: yilingchung27@gmail.com
Website: https://yilingchung.github.io/
Yi-Ling Chung is a Senior research scientist at Genaios. Her work addresses misinformation and online harms through fact-checking, abuse detection, and response generation, and investigates the impact of new AI techniques on online safety. She co-organised the Workshop

Proceedings of the 63rd Annual Meeting of the Association for Computational Linguistics (Volume 5: Tutorial Abstracts), pages 9–10
July 27, 2025

on CounterSpeech for Online Harms, and the Workshop on Online Abuse and Harms (WOAH 7 and 8).

Gavin Abercrombie, Assistant Professor, Heriot-Watt University, Edinburgh, Scotland.
Email: g.abercrombie@hw.ac.uk
Website: https://gavinabercrombie.github.io
Gavin Abercrombie is an Assistant Professor in the Interaction Lab at Heriot-Watt University. His research focuses on socio-technical issues and human aspects of NLP. He is Co-Investigator on the EPSRC project Equally Safe Online, and is a founding organiser of both the workshops on Counterspeech for Online abuse (CS4OA) and Perspectivist Approaches to NLP (NLPerspectives).

Marco Guerini, head of the Language and Dialogue Technologies group at Fondazione Bruno Kessler (FBK), Italy.
Email: m.guerini@fbk.eu
Website: https://www.marcoguerini.eu
Marco Guerini is the head of the Language and Dialogue Technologies group at FBK. He works on NLP for persuasive communication, sentiment analysis and social media. In recent years his research has focused on the development of generative AI technologies to fight online hate and misinformation. He is the coordinator of EU funded projects, author of scientific publications in top-level conferences and international journals and organiser of workshops and shared tasks.

(2) Invited Speakers:

Cathy Buerger, Director of Research at the Dangerous Speech Project.
Email: cathy@dangerousspeech.org
Website: https://cathybuerger.com/
Dr. Cathy Buerger is the Director of Research at the Dangerous Speech Project where her work is dedicated to understanding and mitigating harmful speech and its role in inciting violence. She is a Research Affiliate of the University of Connecticut's Economic and Social Rights Research Group and Managing Editor of the Journal of Human Rights. She holds a PhD in Anthropology from the University of Connecticut.

Simone Fontana, journalist, managing editor of Facta.
Email: s.fontana@facta.news
Website: https://muckrack.com/simone-fontana1
Simone Fontana is a journalist based in Italy and managing editor of Facta. He focuses on disinformation, politics, extremism and online communities, but he also covered social and economic issues related to the environmental and climate crisis. His work has been published in Italy and abroad in publications such as La Repubblica, L'Espresso, Domani, Wired, Rolling Stone, Green European Journal and The Daily Dot.

Synthetic Data in the Era of Large Language Models

Vijay Viswanathan, Xiang Yue, Alisa Liu, Yizhong Wang and Graham Neubig

Website: https://synth-data-acl.github.io/

Progress in natural language processing has historically been driven by better data, and researchers today are increasingly using "synthetic data" - data generated with the assistance of large language models - to make dataset construction faster and cheaper. However, most synthetic data generation approaches are executed in an ad hoc manner and "reinvent the wheel" rather than build on prior foundations. This tutorial seeks to build a shared understanding of recent progress in synthetic data generation from NLP and related fields by grouping and describing major methods, applications, and open problems. Our tutorial will be divided into four main sections. First, we will describe algorithms for producing high-quality synthetic data. Second, we will describe how synthetic data can be used to advance the general-purpose development and study of language models. Third, we will demonstrate how to customize synthetic data generation to support scenario-specific applications. Finally, we will discuss open questions about the production and use of synthetic data that must be answered to overcome some of their current limitations. Our goal is that by unifying recent advances in this emerging research direction, we can build foundations upon which the community can improve the rigor, understanding, and effectiveness of synthetic data moving forward.

Vijay Viswanathan, PhD Student, Carnegie Mellon University
Email: vijayv@andrew.cmu.edu
Website: https://www.cs.cmu.edu/ vijayv

Vijay is a PhD student at Carnegie Mellon University, where he works with Sherry Tongshuang Wu and Graham Neubig. He is interested in making AI models more reliable at following specifications of behavior (e.g. task descriptions or instructions), primarily by using synthetic data to achieve this goal. His research received an Outstanding Demo Paper award at ACL 2022 and he received an NEC Student Research Fellowship in 2022.

Xiang Yue, Postdoctoral Fellow, Carnegie Mellon University
Email: xyue2@andrew.cmu.edu
Website: https://xiangyue9607.github.io/

Xiang Yue is a postdoctoral fellow at Carnegie Mellon University, specializing in natural language processing (NLP). His work focuses on advancing the reasoning capabilities of large language models (LLMs) through a data-centric approach. Xiang's research has earned several awards, including a Best Paper Finalist recognition at CVPR 2024, a Best Paper Honorable Mention at ACL 2023, and a Best Paper Award at IEEE BIBM 2021, all centered around (synthetic) data generation. He was also a recipient of the Carnegie Bosch Postdoctoral Fellowship and was recognized as a rising star at the 2024 UMASS Generative AI Workshop.

Alisa Liu, PhD Student, University of Washington
Email: alisaliu@cs.washington.edu
Website: https://alisawuffles.github.io/

Alisa Liu is a PhD student at the University of Washington, working with Yejin Choi and Noah Smith. Her research interests includes developing algorithms for text generation, particularly as a tool for data creation. She is supported by the NSF Graduate Research Fellowship and OpenAI SuperAlignment Fellowship.

Yizhong Wang, PhD Student, University of Washington
Email: yizhongw@cs.washington.edu

Proceedings of the 63rd Annual Meeting of the Association for Computational Linguistics (Volume 5: Tutorial Abstracts), pages 11–12
July 27, 2025 ©2025 Association for Computational Linguistics

Website: https://homes.cs.washington.edu/ yizhongw/
Yizhong Wang is a PhD student at the University of Washington, advised by Hannaneh Hajishirzi and Noah Smith. He is also a student researcher at the Allen Institute for Artificial Intelligence (AI2), working on building open language models. His research focuses on the fundamental data challenges in AI development and algorithms centered around data. He has won multiple paper awards, including ACL 2024 Best Theme Paper, CCL 2020 Best Paper, and ACL 2017 Outstanding Paper. He was the co-organizer of the Student Research Workshop at ACL 2020 and the Instruction Tuning and Instruction Following Workshop at NeurIPS 2023.

Graham Neubig, Associate Professor, Carnegie Mellon University
Email: gneubig@cs.cmu.edu
Website: https://www.phontron.com/
Graham Neubig is an associate professor at the Language Technologies Institute of Carnegie Mellon University. His research focuses on natural language processing, with a particular interest in fundamentals, applications, and understanding of large language models for tasks such as question answering, code generation, and multilingual applications. He has published over 270 papers in *ACL venues, and won 5 best paper or honorable mention awards. He has taught tutorials at several *ACL conferences, such as a tutorial on neural networks at EMNLP, and a tutorial on code generation at NAACL.

Guardrails and Security for LLMs: Safe, Secure and Controllable Steering of LLM Applications

Traian Rebedea, Leon Derczynski, Shaona Ghosh, Makesh Narsimhan Sreedhar, Faeze Brahman, Liwei Jiang, Bo Li, Yulia Tsvetkov, Christopher Parisien, and Yejin Choi

Website: `https://llm-guardrails-security.github.io/`

Pretrained generative models, especially large language models, provide novel ways for users to interact with computers. While generative NLP research and applications had previously aimed at very domain-specific or task-specific solutions, current LLMs and applications (e.g. dialogue systems, agents) are versatile across many tasks and domains. Despite being trained to be helpful and aligned with human preferences (e.g., harmlessness), enforcing robust guardrails on LLMs remains a challenge. And, even when protected against rudimentary attacks, just like other complex software, LLMs can be vulnerable to attacks using sophisticated adversarial inputs. This tutorial provides a comprehensive overview of key guardrail mechanisms developed for LLMs, along with evaluation methodologies and a detailed security assessment protocol - including auto red-teaming of LLM-powered applications. Our aim is to move beyond the discussion of single prompt attacks and evaluation frameworks towards addressing how guardrailing can be done in complex dialogue systems that employ LLMs.

Traian Rebedea, Principal Research Scientist at NVIDIA and Associate Professor at University Politehnica of Bucharest.
Email: `trebedea@nvidia.com`
Website: `https://www.linkedin.com/in/trebedea/`
His research is focused mainly on dialogue and safety, on topics such as dialogue steering and improving multi-turn LLM safety and security. At the same time, he is an important contributor in developing Romanian models and datasets. He received his PhD from University Politehnica of Bucharest, Romania. Prior to joining NVIDIA, he co-founded Roboself and was Chief Data Scientist at Wholi, working on dialogue systems and information retrieval.

Leon Derczynski, Principal Research Scientist in LLM Security at NVIDIA, Associate Professor in NLP at ITU University of Copenhagen, & President of ACL SIGSEC.
Email: `lderczynski@nvidia.com`
Website: `https://www.linkedin.com/in/leon-derczynski/`
Prof Derczynski has organised many workshops and tasks in the past (multiple WNUT, multiple TempEval, multiple RumourEval, OffensEval), as well as co-chairing COLING 2018, ACing and SACing all the major ACL events, and EiCing a journal (NEJLT). He has held tutorials at NAACL 2023, COLING 2020, and EACL 2014.

Shaona Ghosh, Senior Research Scientist at NVIDIA.
Email: `shaonag@nvidia.com`
Website: `https://www.linkedin.com/in/shaonaghosh`
Dr Ghosh is Senior Research Scientist at NVIDIA, focusing on AI safety and leading efforts in LLM content moderation. She chairs the AI Risk and Reliability workstream at MLCommons, contributing to its global AI safety benchmark. She completed postdoctoral research at University of Cambridge and University of Oxford, and holds a PhD from the University of Southampton, in collaboration with UCL in the UK. Previously, she worked at Apple for six years on safety, robustness, and privacy in NLP, computer vision, and multimodal domains.

Makesh Narsimhan Sreedhar, Research Scientist at NVIDIA.
Email: `makeshn@nvidia.com`

Proceedings of the 63rd Annual Meeting of the Association for Computational Linguistics (Volume 5: Tutorial Abstracts), pages 13–15
July 27, 2025

Website: https://www.linkedin.com/in/makeshsreedhar/

He is a Research Scientist at NVIDIA, working on AI Safety and model alignment techniques. His current research focuses on enhancing dialogue systems and improving the instruction-following capabilities of language models. He holds a Master's degree from the University of Wisconsin-Madison.

Faeze Brahman, Research Scientist at Allen Institute for AI.
Email: fae.brahman@gmail.com
Website: https://fabrahman.github.io/

She did her Ph.D. in Computer Science at the University of California, Santa Cruz. She is broadly interested in understanding language model's capabilities and limitations. More recently, she focused on AI alignment, trustworthy AI and robust evaluation of LLMs' safety in complex interactive tasks. She has organized multiple workshops at ACL and AAAI as well as AC'ing and SAC'ing major ACL conferences.

Liwei Jiang, PhD Student at the University of Washington and Graduate Research Intern at NVIDIA.
Email: lwjiang@cs.washington.edu
Website: https://liweijiang.github.io/

She is a Ph.D. candidate at Paul G. Allen School of Computer Science & Engineering, University of Washington, advised by Prof Yejin Choi. She is a graduate research intern at NVIDIA and was previously a student researcher at Allen Institute for AI. Her research centers on humanistic AI safety, currently focusing on pluralistic alignment, self-improving algorithms for steerable and secure language models, and anticipatory strategies for long-term risks, such as overreliance and the erosion of human creativity.

Bo Li, Associate Professor in the Department of Computer Science at the University of Illinois at Urbana-Champaign.
Email: bol@uchicago.edu
Website: https://aisecure.github.io/

Prof Li is the recipient of several awards, including the IJCAI Computers and Thought Award, Alfred P. Sloan Research Fellowship, NSF CAREER Award, AI's 10 to Watch, MIT Technology Review TR-35 Award, and also best paper awards at several top machine learning and security conferences. Her research focuses on both theoretical and practical aspects of trustworthy machine learning, which is at the intersection of machine learning, security, privacy, and game theory. She has designed several scalable frameworks for robust learning and privacy-preserving data publishing systems.

Yulia Tsvetkov, Associate Professor at the University of Washington.
Email: yuliats@cs.washington.edu
Website: https://homes.cs.washington.edu/ yuliats/

Prof Tsvetkov is Associate Professor in the Paul G. Allen School of Computer Science & Engineering at the University of Washington. Her work is in natural language processing, with a focus on AI ethics and safety. Her lab develops models and algorithms to advance language technologies for high-stakes domains such as health, science, and education. This research integrates advances in machine learning with novel evaluation and alignment methods to ensure large language models serve diverse users and avoid harm.

Christopher Parisien, Senior Manager of Applied Research at NVIDIA.
Email: cparisien@nvidia.com
Website: https://www.linkedin.com/in/christopher-m-parisien/

Dr Parisien is leading research efforts in safety, security, and dialogue in large language models at NVIDIA. He holds a PhD in Computational Linguistics from the University of Toronto. He has served as a research scientist at Nuance, focused on virtual assistants and clinical language understanding, and as Chief Technology Officer at NexJ Health, a patient-centred health platform.

Yejin Choi, Professor and MacArthur Fellow at Stanford University, and Senior Director at NVIDIA.
Email: yejinc@stanford.edu
Website: https://yejinc.github.io/
Yejin Choi is Dieter Schwarz Foundation Professor of Computer Science and Senior Fellow at Human Centered Artificial Intelligence at Stanford University, Senior Director at NVIDIA, and an ACL Fellow. Prof Choi has presented multiple keynotes and won best and outstanding papers at related venues including NeurIPS and ACL, and held tutorials at ACL 2020, CVPR 2020, and COLING 2022.

Author Index